Liquid
Limericks

Liquid Limericks

Titillation for tipplers

Pictures by Oliver Preston,
Script by Alistair Sampson

ROBSON BOOKS

This paperback edition first published in Great Britain in 2002 by Robson Books,
64 Brewery Road, London N7 9NT

A member of the Chrysalis Group plc

British Library Cataloguing in Publication Data
A catalogue record for this title is available from the British Library.

ISBN 1 86105 543 9

Printed by Butler & Tanner Ltd.,
London and Frome

(25.6.03)c.

Foreword

No question about it, Alistair is the wittiest fellow of my acquaintance. Moreover, we share the same sense of humour which verges on blue. As for limericks, he vies with my wife whose memory is so much better than mine (and her humour positively violet). But it is my fault really. Sometime in the mid 1950s on a visit to Bordeaux I sneaked into a bookshop which, at the time, was next door to the now defunct Café de Bordeaux, opposite the Grand Theatre. In a back corner were avant-garde works published by Olympia Press and in their midst was Count Palmerios Book of Limericks, edited by none other than Christopher Logue, which is why they were not only wickedly wicked but, most essential, the verses scanned perfectly. Moreover the cover was enchanting -- a man gazing with surprise at the sight of a large tulip rising between his outstretched legs. At one time, my wife Daphne and I had only to mention the number of one of the limericks, and we fell about laughing for we knew most of it by heart.

Oliver Preston, in spite of, or maybe because of, a generation gap a mile wide between himself and Alistair, has produced a series of illustrations which perfectly complement the limericks. Although Oliver is one of this country's leading cartoonists and current Chairman of the Cartoon Art Trust, he thrives, as the male voyeur will appreciate, on drawing pretty girls. His work has wit and grace. *Liquid Limericks* is a match made in Heaven.

The other thing that Alistair and I and our respective wives have in common is wine, so for me and I am sure for all wine buffs, here is an irresistible melange of wit and wine.

Michael Broadbent M.W.

Wine Writer of the Year 2001

OLIVER PRESTON

A Girl with Bottle

A second year student at Girton
Was frequently seen with no skirt on.
She said, 'I'm a doll
'Who prefers Pomerol.
'Of that I am Vieux Château Certan.'

God loves a Cheerful Spender

A banker with money to burn
Shouted, 'Bring me a glass of Sauternes –
'The crème de la crème
'Your finest Yquem –
'I might just as well drink what I earn.'

OK, I Give In

A Lothario threatened his squeeze,
As they frolicked around 'neath the trees,
'If you play hard to get
'I shall grab you my pet
'And force feed you with Beaumes-de-Venise.'

OLIVER PRESTON

Beastly Good Taste

Viscount Tipple, a gentleman farmer,
Entirely agreed with his llama.
They placed an embargo
On all other Margaux,
But thought Palmer an absolute charmer.

OLIVER PRESTON

Out of Kilter

A Scots lass, one Mistress McCarten,
Led a life that was sober and spartan;
But she'd push out the boat
Once a week; down her throat
Went a magnum of Léoville-Barton.

All Scotties Drink Too Much

They knew Claud had gone a bit potty
When he started to hoard Aligoté.
He would cry, 'Bless my soul!'
And pour some in the bowl
Of MacPherson, his favourite scotty.

One Great Year, One Great Idea

A lass, if plied with Châteauneuf,
Will willy-nilly hit the turf.
You can have great fun
With a sixty-one;
But more with a soixante-neuf.

PRESTON

More Thirsty Than Hungary

A Scotsman emerged from the loo
To find a young Magyar in view
'I just canna think
'Why you're here – have a drink.
'I expect you'll want Tokay the noo.'

Pure Gold

'Do have a sip,' I began,
'Just a very small sip if you can.
'Don't think me mean,
'But I'd better come clean
'The name of the wine is Le Pin.'

Mud in Your Eye

A very well-spoken young blood
Was wrestling a girl in the mud.
As they rolled in the slime
He remarked, 'I'm part-time
'With Berry Brothers and Rudd.'

Taking it With You

An oenophile based in Torquay
Gave up sex when he hit 93.
'But I'd never abandon
'My Möet and Chandon
'In my will I have left it to me.'

OLIVER PRESTON

Cornish Cream

A head-hunter based in St Ives
Disposed of a series of wives.
Had good sense, had this murderer.
He served Louis Roederer,
So his wives had the deaths of their lives.

Basso Profundo

A barmaid with pretty blue eyes
Pulled pints much more often than guys;
Then a brewer called Bass
Caught sight of the lass
And gave her a lovely surprise.

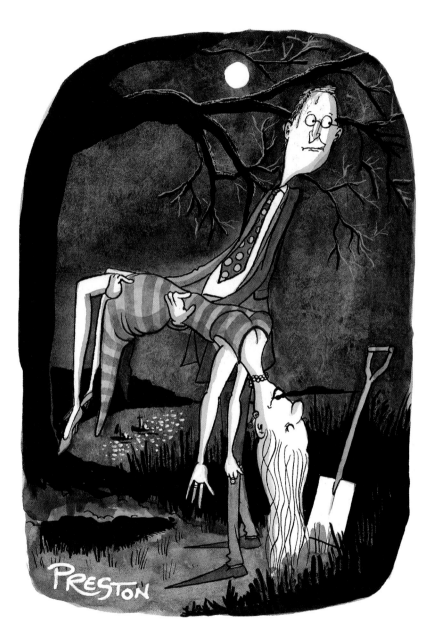

Toujours la Politesse

Do smoke while you drink my Latour.
That is just what a first growth is for.
It's a pity to waste it
Even though you can't taste it.
But wouldn't you rather have Pouilly-Fumé instead?

In the Pink

A spinster from Southend-on-Sea
Was oenocologically twee.
She often would say
Of her pink négligee,
'It's my dear little Côtes de Nuit.'

The Drinking Classes

Old Labour used to drink shandy
But that's not for Tony and Mandy.
Tony who's heterous
Always drinks Pétrus
While randy old Mandy drinks brandy.

In Tents

Hiawatha observed to his squaw
Minnehaha, 'The wines of Cahors
'Are extremely intense
'Just like us in one sense.'
And let out an enormous guffaw

OLIVER PRESTON

OLIVER PRESTON

Very Cross Channel

Dear Archie,
We went on a cruise
'Cross the Channel in search of cheap booze.
Easy trip - Eurotunnels
Stacked the car to the gunwhales
Broke the axle.
Love Jane.

(No more news).

Monkey Business

Said Amanda, a peach of a girl,
'I go ape if I drink Cantemerle.'
Her ape said, 'Amanda,
'May I speak with candour?
'I have some. Let's give it a whirl.'

Lily of Lagune

A Frenchman looked up at the moon
And said, 'Zey are playing our tune.'
His friend Lily, she said,
'Eet has gone to my 'ead,
'Pas la lune, pas la tune, mais Lagune.'

Roll out the Barolo

Pavarotti, I'm told, is quite anti
The concept of Asti Spumante –
But give him Barolo
And he'll sing you a solo
Extolling the charms of Chianti.

Knowing His Spanish Onions

When a Spaniard I know cries, 'Olé!'
What can his wife do but obey?
After several Riojas
He tickles her knockers
And then has his Iberian way.

OLIVER PRESTON

OLIVER PRESTON

Over the Hill

There once was a stripper called Fleur
Who could hardly be termed 'en primeur'.
Tho' she spent her life tannin'
She could not get a man in.
Perhaps she was corked, as it were?

Chuckèd

Chuck used to be frightfully dapper
Before he found out about Grappa.
Now from here to eternity
It's bye-bye fraternity
Adio to pi-betta-kappa.

At Your Service

I *never* would drink Bechevelle
In a restaurant or a hotel.
I dislike wasting loot,
But if, dear old fruit,
You're paying do give me a bell.

Horses for Courses

There was a young filly called Fanny
Who gave vin de table to her nanny.
With a beau worth a billion,
They imbibed St Emilion,
With a nice Pontet-Canet for granny.

A Bit Rich

I think I will always remember
When Kev made his pile last November
'Give them Nouveau all round'
You could not hear a sound
From the club that had made him a member.

On the Rocks

A steward on board the Titanic
As she sank said, 'Milady don't panic
'It's the lifeboats for you -
'Leave your Branaire Ducru,
'Which frankly Your Grace is too tannic.'

OLIVER PRESTON

Barrow Boy

'My dear have a drop of this Tawny,'
Said Charles, 'oh I do feel so horny.
'I have never felt sexier,
'Now excuse my dyslexia,
'But I'm working for Barrow and Corney.'

Grey Hairs

As Percival Plonker grew older
His bouquet quite tended to moulder.
He had much madderise,
Than most other guys
And was quite often ullaged to shoulder.

OLIVER PRESTON

Whoops

We once had a bit of a party,
Mixing Advocaat, Rum and Frascati
With fried eggs - a blunder -
It was frankly no wonder
That you never heard chunder so hearty.

Hip Flasks at Noon

Upon the killing fields, our host
Mid-morning stops to drink a toast.
'To those we injure.'
One downs King's Ginger
Before returning to one's post.

Do You Smokie afterwards?

A newly wed lad from Arbroath,
Just after he plighted his troth,
Murmured, 'Flora my sweet,
'Let us try some Lafite.
'I hope you enjoy my first growth.'

A Better Class of Brylcreem

I shall never forget dear old Pa;
He was happiest propping a bar.
With his nice cheery face –
Not a hair out of place –
All thanks to his favourite Pommard.

Tory Story

A conservative lover called Leon
Was fond of a glass of Haut Brion.
His girlfriend's position
Was always La Mission –
She wasn't as pretty as Ffion.

OLIVER PRESTON

Two's Company

While Jane had a douche on her own
Will arrived, so she wasn't alone.
With a kiss on the bouche
He produced Clos des Mouches
And she cried, 'That's a bit near the Beaune.'

Stuffed Prune

Prunella was perfectly pure.
Quite depressingly dull and demure.
Then Rupert the rotter
Grabbed hold of and got her
With a gallon of Calon-Ségur.

Scotch Missed

A whisky buff sat in his chair
And called the sommelier there.
'While the Grouse that I drink
'Has no need to be pink
'I do like my J & B rare.'

OLIVER PRESTON

OLIVER PRESTON

Lucky Jim

Hooray! There's a party at Jim's.
What a riot! He always serves Pimms.
It's a bundle of fun
With his Pimms No. 1.
He's from Essex but lives in South Mimms.

Abstinence Makes the Heart Grow Fonder

Luke spent each Lent on the wagon
And said, 'My, how the time seems to drag on.
'Pellegrino and Perrier
'Don't make a man merrier.
'Bring me Easter and bring me a flagon.'

Hard Opus

There once was a beauty called Sally.
They voted her Miss Napa Valley.
Then she married. Their son
They named 'Opus One'
By Opus Fifteen they'd lost tally.

Amazing Grace

Tho' her hairs were a little bit grey
She had legs and a charming bouquet.
She also was graced
With a long aftertaste
And she certainly went all the way.

Holiday Postcard

This one's of me and the chaps.
Those are fräuleins we've got on our laps.
I know what you're thinking
Quite right; we'd been drinking.
We call these our holiday Schnapps.

Truly Scrumptious

She was not a bit dumpy or frumpy.
Where it mattered the most she was lumpy.
What a girl about town!
What a joy to lay down!
What a marvellous mouthful of Scrumpy!

OLIVER
PRESTON

A Purple Passage

Uncle Willoughby used to go puce
If he strayed far from pineapple juice.
He was really quite naughty
To auntie, his forte
Was pure alcoholic abuse.

The Cogniscenti

With Mabel, I'll cruise down the Rhine.
Now, she knows I'm a Master of Wine
I shall glance at the label,
Take a sip and cry 'Mabel
'If you ask me this brandy is Hine.'

OLIVER PRESTON

Exchanging Contracts

A chartered surveyor, an ass,
Came across a commodious lass.
For months he surveyed her
And then, when he'd laid her,
He conveyed her a case (of Las Cases).

Dying for a Drink

I was spending the weekend at Eth's.
In *The Times* we were scanning the deaths.
I said 'Eth, dear old friend,
'If you want to extend
'Your life, then ease up on the meths.'

Royal Flush

Let loose in the royal enclosure
Piers totally lost his composure.
After far too much Meursault
He came over queer, so
What happened? A flash of exposure.

Console-ation

Miss Toccata, a bit of a gorgon,
Was playing a fugue on the organ;
Then she pulled out the stops
And had quite a few drops
Of a passable vintage of Morgon.

Bearing All

There once was a koala
With a penchant for Marsala.
He would knock it back
And then make track
For the nearest massage parlour.

OLIVER PRESTON

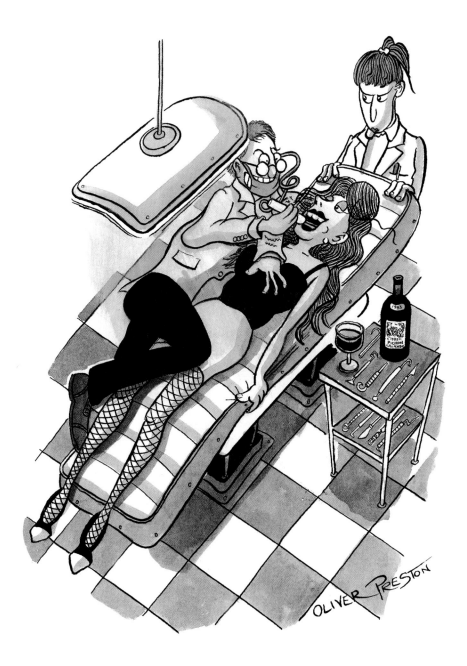

OLIVER PRESTON

A Bridge Too Far

A dentist was deep into drilling
A modern young miss who was willing.
'Do,' he said, 'Hold my hand.
'Try some Pichon-Lalande
'While I finish your root canal filling.'

X RAY 152·17·

OLIVER PRESTON

Camping Out

St John, a lovable ponce,
Retired, and decamped to Provence,
Where he quite often chose a
Precocious young rosé
Which he kept lightly chilled in two fonts.

OLIVER PRESTON

Coming on Strong

The wine buff was striking a pose.
'Why this has a flirtatious nose.
'As it's somewhat retroussé,
'Quite frankly would you say
'It's a skittish young Gruaud-Larose?'

Mark Up

Said the waiter, our 'Entre-Deux-Mers
'Is just riddled with devil may care.
'When back it you've tossed
'At just five times our cost
'It's goodbye to a wing and a prayer.'

Foster Child

A very young lady from Gloucester
Once longed for a bottle of Foster.
They offered her Harp.
She said, 'Sorry to carp
'That's not Foster, that's just an imposter.'

Down the Hatch

A bald undertaker called Harve
Was quite indescribably suave.
He would not say a word
While the stiff was interred,
But unearthed a half bottle of Graves.

OLIVER PRESTON

Wine Firm

A keen young director of Avery
Kept his female assistant in slavery.
He murmured, 'I'm fond,
'But you must stay in bond –
'That's the way that I find you most savoury.'

Down Under

Between Sydney and Melbourne, a jogger
Saw a Sheila - felt minded to snog her;
They drank in a bar a
Superb Coonawarra
And XXXX when they reached Wagga Wagga.

Hectoring Hector

A sadist who lived in Saltash
Was extremely adept with the lash.
He would flog poor old Hector,
A keen wine collector,
And then he would flog his La Tâche.

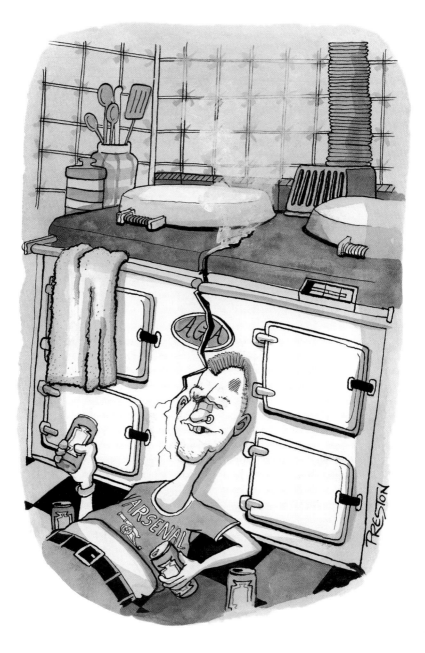

Why Darren Missed the Football Match

I really must tell you the saga
Of the lout who could not hold his lager.
He drank several gallons
Then quite lost his balance
And fractured himself and the Aga.

Doggy Bottle

There once was a naughty old fag
Who, when dining with chums used to brag
That, if offered Latour,
He would secretly pour
Some in his colostomy bag.

The Hand that Feeds You

Mr Pratt is a bad tempered cat,
Who is also as blind as a bat.
If you feed him, he'll bite
Your hand with delight,
So I beg you do not a Noilly Prat.

OLIVER PRESTON

OLIVER PRESTON

Nipped in the Bud

A beautiful blonde called Eliza
Had a boyfriend who liked to surprise her.
This stud, name of Bud
Gave her diamonds - all dud.
So she ditched him - and that made Budweiser.

Ma Sherry

While acting in the Mikado
I spotted Brigitte Bardot.
She was licking a Walls
At the front of the stalls
And sipping Amontillado.

Hock Aye The Noo

'I think you'll like this Eiswein'
Said Hans, 'It is a nice wine.'
'I pick the grapes on Christmas morn
'With a yuletide toot on my alpenhorn
'That's why it's a high price wine.'

PRESTON

Imperfect Bed Fellows

A bottle of le Montrachet
Retains a certain cachet.
It goes with sole,
But on the whole
Not with bangers and mash, eh?

When you drink with the Devil

When the time came for Cecil to pass on
His wife at the wake drank Paul Masson.
Now Cecil's in Hell
Where they drink Hirondelle
And Gallo is greatly in fashion.

Not Something to Passover

I was not far from having a fit, sir,
While drinking at Maurie's Barmitzvah.
'Twas Le Pez '61,
Then some son of a gun
Insisted on having a spritzer.

Favourite Allergy

I am sorry to let off steam,
But there's one thing makes me scream.
It's not Princess Anne –
I'm rather a fan –
It's Bailey's Irish Cream.

Rum Do

When Nelson's fate was ill-starred, he
Never said, 'Kiss me Hardy.'
What he actually said,
Just before he was dead,
Was, 'No, I said a Bacardi.'

Sheep that Pass in the Night

When going to sleep I count mouton
Or pheasants, should there be a shoot on.
If I still cannot sleep
I watch some Stag's Leap.
Now that's something I'd spend hard-earned loot on.

You Can't Start Too Young

As the vicar stood by the font, he
Christened the little lad Monty.
Then they drove home full throttle
And filled up his bottle
With the very best Romanée-Conti.

Money Isn't Everything

I said to the missus, 'Oh gosh,
'We are really quite low on the dosh.
'Bye bye prestige cuvée,
'Let us jump 'neath our duvet
'And go wild as we drink Stellenbosch.'

Sal Volatile

An au pair called Sarah kept happy
With a very large créme de menthe frappé
Then she'd knock back three gins
And remark to the twins,
'Would you each change the other one's nappy?'

Tied House

A lesbian lady from Luton
Used to walk round her home with one boot on.
She would tie up her friend
And then peacefully spend
The whole afternoon drinking Mouton.

From Russia With Love

Should gin on the breath cause a turn off
Then offer your friends only Smirnoff,
Or try Absolut;
But were I, my friend, you
I would let half the alcohol burn off.

Gotcha

An aging young lady called Betty
Got married and stood on a jetty
She said, 'Thank God I'm spliced
'Get the Bollinger iced
'While I cover myself in confetti.'

High Jinks

Sophia, a Tuscan Contessa,
Got hitched to a eunuch, God bless her.
'Let us drink Amoretto,'
Sang he. His falsetto
Quite quickly began to depress her.

Why Get into Hock?

My very good friend Lady Cayzer
Asked 'Who is the damn fool who paysa
Price so handsome –
A monarch's ransom
For a Trochenbeerenauslese?'

Wine taken in excessive doses
Causes depression and cirrhosis –
While wine imbibed in moderation
Helps the heart and spreads elation.

We hope this tome has entertained you
And that the ditties have not drained you.
Young men may well have palpitations
On studying the illustrations.

May everyone enjoy the frolics
Devised by we two alcoholics!

Alistair Sampson   Oliver Preston